TABLE OF CONTENTS

OVERVIEW

UNDERSTANDING THE I-SPEAK YOUR LANGUAGE® COMMUNICATION SYSTEM

THE I-SPEAK YOUR LANGUAGE® SYSTEM

The I-SPEAK® communication system on which the content of this manual is focused centers around the theories of Carl Jung, a noted Swiss psychologist. Jung's work holds that there are preferences towards extroversion and introversion in our personalities which influence the ways in which we process information and, thereby, communicate.

The I-SPEAK Survey indicates that there are four major personality styles which normal individuals can use in their approach to work and life. The emphasis given to a particular style is based on the degree to which the individual chooses any given approach over another.

The I-SPEAK Survey recognizes that while each of us may favor a primary style, no one uses a single style in a vacuum. Therefore, I-SPEAK is designed to measure the relative likelihood of one's using any of the four major styles. The styles are described in light of their behavioral activities as follows:

Style	Behavioral Function
INTUITOR	Conceiving, projecting, inducing
THINKER	Analyzing, ordering in logical fashion
FEELER	Relating to and understanding experience through emotional reactions and responses to feelings
SENSER	Experiencing mainly on the basis of one's own sensory perceptions

A clearer understanding of how individuals experience things and behave is likely if we know the primary and back-up styles of the individual. This knowledge can be acquired by careful observation of one's behavior as well as a review of Section II in this manual entitled "Determining Your Primary and Back-up Style and the Effects of Stress on Each." Of particular value will be understanding how style changes may be experienced under normal conditions as well as under stress conditions.

In and of itself, no style can be considered "good" or "bad." No style is preferred or more "right" than another. Whether a given style should be considered positive or negative depends upon its use under normal and/or stress conditions.

SECTION I
IDENTIFYING THE FOUR MAJOR STYLES

INTUITOR
Overview of Intuitor Type

Intuitor types place high value on ideas, innovation, concepts, theories and long-range thinking. They tend to derive their greatest satisfaction from considering the world of possibilities. Often their imaginative inputs serve as a catalyst for those around them. Intuitors tend to challenge, not because they want to be negative or hostile, but rather because they have learned the value of continuous probing and reexamination. The Intuitor is more stimulated and personally rewarded by effort in problem solving, rather than by implementing solutions.

Occupations Conducive to Intuitor Types

Teachers, artists, writers, planners, policy makers, those who serve on boards and "idea people" are frequently found among Intuitor types. Regardless of their jobs, a person who extensively employs this style is stimulated by intellectual and creative problem-solving endeavors.

For community service, these people may often be encountered playing active roles on boards, task forces, planning committees, or agency leadership groups. In such placements, they are able to assist in problem identification, policy-making, putting priorities on issues, program development, coordination of campaigns, and in pulling together the efforts of a variety of groups or functions.

Intuitor Functioning

Intuitors typically function as fast and deep thinkers. They often reveal excellent imaginations. They question themselves as well as others and, therefore, are not accustomed to taking things for granted. They often seem to have the uncanny ability to anticipate, to project, to, in effect, "know" prior to the time others know. They function as people of vision who have the ability to see relationships between things that others do not comprehend. Sometimes Intuitors are seen as "hard to pin down" or "in a world of their own." Intuitors are deeply interested in the forces of conflicts and theoretical possibilities. Intuitors accept the fact that disorder and chaos are inevitable and are confident in their ability to grasp the meaning of all the conflicts about them.

Intuitors tend to see conflicts in terms of clashes of major forces rather than as here-and-now situations or occurrences. They are inclined to look at the world from the broadest perspective and pride themselves on their ability to see interrelationships between divorced or even abstract parts. They may see others, therefore, who are concerned about the immediate here-and-now, or details, as those who really have missed the importance of "true" issues. They usually resent being placed in situations where they are in any sense "hemmed in" or required to think or operate in a structured, well-defined manner. Intuitors enjoy creating their own structure out of disorder. They excel in integrative tasks and situations demanding a long-term view.

Intuitors are inward-looking. They enjoy deriving meaning from imagination. What they see and know to be the most real is frequently seen by others as unreal and often "impractical."

Positive Traits of Intuitors

When Intuitors are at their best they are seen as leaders and visionaries — people who can cut through the smokescreens of tradition or past practices and focus on the essentials of a situation. They are able to see profitable new directions or solutions of great value that others have missed. Frequently, they bring up fresh and novel approaches and ideas.

Challenges for Intuitors

At their worst, Intuitors may be seen "long on vision, short on action." They may avoid some of the tedious nitty gritty. They may be so convinced of the power and value of their insights and contributions that they may not see the necessity of documenting or proving them to the satisfaction of others. In fact, they may seem impatient and irritated with others who demand detailed evidence or do not see the value of their ideas as they do. Therefore, Intuitors may be criticized for being overly abstract or theoretical. Sometimes, at their worst, Intuitors may be seen as acting "superior" or being condescending in their communications.

Intuitor Functioning Under Stress

When Intuitors are under stress, they run the risk of being seen by others as detached or overly intellectualized. They will be seen as quite indifferent to the reality of the situation and may even be seen as ego-centered or living in an "Ivory Tower." At times, under stress, Intuitors can become quite rigid, uncompromising and impractical. They may appear to be more concerned with the development and defense of their ideas than in translating them into more usable forms or trying to adapt them to the inputs made by others. They are apt to care more that they are satisfied with an approach that is conceptually sound rather than testing it or helping others to gain from it in a utilitarian fashion.

Intuitor Time Orientation

Intuitors are more interested in what should be done in the future than in what has been done in the past. They are more interested in and committed to change than in analyzing past events or modifying the immediate situation. Since they gain great satisfaction from the world of ideas and imagination, they excel in projecting possibilities into the future. For Intuitors, the world of the possible is the most "real" and satisfying. They live and derive satisfaction in terms of the future.

Environmental Clues to Intuitor Type

• Desk: Piled with books and papers (particularly those of theoretical or survey variety). Evidence of lots of projects going on at once.

• Office: Abstract paintings on the wall. Surrounding likely to be imaginative and perhaps avant garde or different. A round table is likely. Clutter.

• Dress: Not very fashion conscious. May reflect a look of the "absent-minded professor." Not concerned with ways in which they present themselves. If concerned with fashion at all, the clothing may be stylish and even exotic.

THINKER
Overview of Thinker Type

Thinker types place high value on logic, ideas and systematic inquiry. They like to identify a problem, develop a variety of possible solutions, weigh the solutions carefully and test the solutions to see that the most logical, systematic approach is followed.

Occupations Conducive to Thinker Types

Lawyers, engineers, scientists, technicians, financially oriented business personnel, systems analysts and administrators are often found among Thinker types.

Thinker Functioning

Thinkers generally function in a steady, tenacious manner. They rely on their observation and rational principles and avoid emotionalism and speculation. They are often skeptical toward the novel, at least until new ideas have been thoroughly analyzed, tested and reviewed in the light of other possible alternatives. They are often skeptical about their own initial reactions to things as well as to the initial reactions and formulations of others. Thinkers would rather "sleep" on an idea and review it carefully before taking a position or making a commitment than to just "go" with the ideas. They avoid being swept along by the needs of the moment.

Thinkers are often seen as very consistent producers. They are logical result-getters as opposed to individuals who are primarily visionary or idea people. Thinkers may be valued for their prudence and thoughtful analysis rather than for their skill in mobilizing the enthusiasm of others.

Thinkers are often sought after for their objectivity and cool thinking under pressure. They usually have good ability to develop logical methods which enable others to test alternatives and to select logically among them.

Positive Traits of Thinkers

At their best, Thinkers may be seen as a consistent force for progress (thinkers as well as doers). They are able to cut through smokescreens of untested ideas and emotional fervor. Thinkers can be highly effective in organizing themselves and others to research and plan. Therefore, they are of great assistance in executing a logical, painstaking and profitable project.

Challenges for Thinkers

At their worst, Thinkers may be seen as overly cautious and conservative. They may emphasize deliberation and thereby de-emphasize action. They may get so bogged down in the weighing, checking, testing and researching that others perceive them as indecisive. Sometimes Thinkers will be seen as stumbling blocks to action that represents a departure from tradition. When they try to deal with change, basing their actions on rational principles, they may be viewed as rigid and dogmatic. Thinkers may be criticized for being mechanistic or impersonal. Sometimes people see them as nonspontaneous or "dry" and "cold."

Thinker Functioning Under Stress

When Thinkers are under stress they usually rely too heavily on their style and run the risk of being seen as rigid, overly cautious and insecure. While they may be viewed as being anxious to proceed, they will not do so at the expense of much risk. They are more concerned with their correct assessments than with the resourceful and timely exploitation of opportunities. When their associates feel under pressure, they may seem quite disinterested in the human feelings of those around them and "out of touch" in the sense that they may seem to be naively idealistic.

Thinker Time Orientation

Thinkers look at time from all dimension: past, present and future. They see them as equally important. Thinkers typically are less concerned with making the so-called dramatic breakthrough than in correctly and consistently relating a present course of action to both the past and the future. It is difficult for Thinkers to deviate from their position of looking at a problem from the dimensions of the past, present and future. To do so might propel them forward into the unknown, speculative world of the Intuitor, push them back to the emotion-based memories of the Feeler's past or overly orient them to the Senser's preoccupation with immediate experiences in the present.

While time is a logical progression, the Thinker is not as concerned with specific events as with the process of progression of experience. Thinkers pride themselves on continuing to learn and extend the framework of their thinking.

Environmental Clues to Thinker Type

- Desk: Neat and orderly with only those things in view that she/he is currently working on. Looks efficient and effective.

- Office: Likely to be organized and uncluttered. Charts and graphs on the wall or on display. Evidence of computer printouts. Furnishings tasteful and conventional.

- Dress: Neatly dressed. Careful attention to detail such as color coordination and accessories. Conservative, subdued. Ties with geometrical design. For women: understated, well tailored, nothing exotic.

FEELER
Overview of Feeler Type

Feeler types are individuals who place high value on human interaction. They seek and enjoy the stimulation of contact with others and try to understand and analyze their own emotions and the emotions of others. Their concern for and understanding of people usually makes them astute in "reading between the lines" about what people say and do.

Occupations Conducive to Feeler Types

Among Feeler types one might find entertainers, sales people, public relations specialists, health care professionals and counselors.

Whether in their job in society or in their volunteer activities, Feelers are attracted by jobs and situations in which social-interpersonal contacts with others are highly likely. Feelers are sought after in groups or individually for their ability to listen, empathize and for their patience and forbearance in carrying assistance to others experiencing troubles or crises in their lives.

Feeler Functioning

Feelers are likely to be perceived as dynamic and stimulating. They are likely to be "warm" and closely in touch with others. They usually function in ways that demonstrate ability to be sensitive to the needs and wants of others. Feelers are able to note discrepancies between speech and expression or between outward behavior and inward feeling. They are sensitive to their own motives and to the motives of others. Feelers are often seen as perceptive and insightful. Others seek them for their ability to sort out complex emotional problems and situations, to interpret the meanings of behavior, or to assess the climate or morale of a group. They are likely to be effective in anticipating or predicting the way others may respond or react to a projected change or action.

Positive Traits of Feelers

At their best, Feelers are likely to be truly perceptive and aware. They are skilled in communication, patient, practical listeners and observers. Often they are able to read and assess organizational politics with accuracy and insight. They are people who can position and see change in ways that reduce resisting forces "before the fact" and thus increase the likelihood of cooperation, teamwork and progress.

Challenges for Feelers

Feelers may be seen as individuals who are more concerned with the process of interaction than with the content of action around which the interacting takes place. They may be seen as having less interest in developing concepts, plans or programs (or in systematically getting them to function) than they do in analyzing, communicating and interpreting whatever is taking place. They rely less on logic and thought than on "gut feel" for the way people and things emotionally strike them. At their worst, they may appear more preoccupied with making an emotional impact on others or persuading them to move, than being concerned as to whether or not such movements have been thought out or carefully planned. Feelers seem to take their own emotional reactions and what they infer others feel as representing "fact." They may act on the basis of their feelings. Sometimes they are seen as defensive and over-reactive and others may criticize them for their subjectivity.

Feelers may be criticized for their emotionalism which may be seen as a substitute for action. They may be seen as somewhat indifferent to tradition and custom and perhaps even cavalier about details or prudent measures valued by others. Under pressure they may be viewed as "thin-skinned" and over-reactive. They may overstep their desire to be bold and outspoken or dramatic and play to the gallery — possibly lacking humility or good sense. Under stress their moods may fluctuate quite widely — reacting to the feelings of the moment — causing somewhat uneven or possibly erratic behavior. Sometimes this causes others to question their credibility.

Feeler Time Orientation

Feelers are more oriented to the past than to other dimensions of time. It is through their ability to draw on past experience and emotional interplay that makes them feel they can make the present meaningful to themselves and to others. As Feelers age they are likely to demonstrate evidence of a unique sentimentality. It becomes increasingly important to them that they be able to relate present experience to significant past memories. Thus, as memories rooted in the past assume increasing influence on present behavior Feelers may be perceived by others as becoming somewhat conservative. This is quite ironic in as much as their general mode is not of this nature.

Environmental Clues to Feeler Type

- Desk: Personal memorabilia (photos, meaningful paperweight, family pictures) and also business papers on desk.

- Office: Like desk, the office will be personalized. On wall, photos of company outing, souvenirs, documents of personal information, awards. Books probably autographed and people-oriented. Tone is of warmth and color.

- Dress: Casual and colorful, yet conventional. Feelers try to make an impression and care about the way they and others look.

SENSER
Overview of Senser Type

Senser types are individuals who place high value on action. They thrive on getting things done here and now, without unnecessary and time-consuming deliberations. They want to implement whatever they believe should be done and they see the actions of others as evidence of their commitment. They believe in the significance of what they and others are doing each day and, therefore, must exploit, in constructive ways, the opportunities for satisfaction that each day affords. They are likely to express a direct, down-to-earth, energetic approach to work and life.

Occupations Conducive to Senser Types

Sensers will frequently be found in marketing, construction, line management and professional athletics. Regardless of their job placement, Sensers tend to be pragmatically-oriented and enjoy making things happen. They engage in activities that provide them with opportunities for concrete, tangible and imme- diate feedback. Because their approach is action-oriented and down-to-earth, they are frequently valued as being the driving force within an organization. Sensers can be constructively relentless in their pursuit of measurable and high quality results. They are often sought after for their drive and ability to translate ideas into products, sales and profits. While Sensers may also be idea-oriented, they tend not to respect an idea until they have seen it translated into something practical and workable.

Senser Functioning

Sensers are doers. They are people who move ahead resourcefully and determinedly. Sometimes they appear to move insurmountable obstacles out of the way. They thrive on working on a wide variety of projects and tasks at once, yet they also demonstrate what seems to be an incredible amount of attention to detail. Sensers are likely to ask themselves the questions — "Will it work? How?" — when considering a new project, proposal or business venture.

Sensers feel comfortable about committing to undertakings only after they have been able to prove to themselves that the proposed action is likely to work. If they cannot understand a proposed action in terms of their direct experience (Who will do what? How? For what purpose? How will we know it is accomplished?) then they may find it difficult or undesirable to proceed further with the matter. This is so because they tend to learn best, not on a conceptual or theoretical basis, but on the basis of immediate, direct, personal experience. For example, if someone is discussing a potentially dramatic breakthrough in computer software, they are likely to interrupt to ask about packaging possibilities or variety of applications.

Sensers will usually be seen as decisive. Quick decision-making is important to Sensers because taking action is one of their primary means of relieving anxiety or preventing wasted time from occurring. When there is indecision, they want to do something and are inclined to take action, even if only on a trial basis, to see if it works and, if so, how. They tend to be more concerned with assessing their own growth and progress (and, perhaps, that of others) in very specific and measurable terms of criteria. That is, they will frequently look for items such as sales volume, quarterly profits, percentage of rejects, etc., than more theoretical or speculative criteria.

Positive Traits of Sensers

Sensers are likely to be seen as dynamic, "herculean" workers who, once having committed themselves to a task, will move mountains to make the undertaking a success. They are seen as growth-oriented, resourceful, well organized, pragmatic, hard-driving. Sensers usually impose high standards of utility on themselves and others. To this degree, they are likely to be seen as constructively impatient or tireless. Sometimes people see them as spirited and down-to-earth, able to convey a sense of mission and purpose to others.

At their best, Sensers are doers "par excellence," who will not only remain on the practice field after the game to work out and perfect their skills, but who will also work tirelessly to coach the less skillful on the team to develop their skills as well.

Challenges for Sensers

Sensers may be seen as failing to sufficiently consider the long-range consequences of their actions. That is, they may be so action-oriented that they "short circuit" significant steps in the planning process. Sometimes they dispense with caution and analysis in a cavalier fashion as though they were saying, "It's the game that counts, so why waste time talking about it or in considering alternatives to the game." They can be criticized for imposing their expectations, drive, high speed and zeal onto others. At their worst, Sensers tend to overemphasize short-time results and act impulsively — trying to drive others to their will — rather than adopting strategies based on the concepts, plans and feelings of others.

Senser Functioning Under Stress

Under stress, the Senser runs the risk of being seen as anti-intellectual, demonstrating tunnel vision, or being defensively overreactive to the differences of opinions that represent resistance for action and movement. Under stress, they can ride roughshod over the feelings of others. Sometimes they fail to assess this impact upon others and are seen as being opinionated and biased. They are likely to construe loyalty as the degree to which others agree with them and help them (even though others may believe them wrong). Under the stress of failures, they may see the lack of success not as a negative reflection of their own style, but as evidence that others are not sufficiently loyal or industrious to make the project work.

Senser Time Orientation

Sensers never want to "spin their wheels" worrying about the past, nor do they try to "crystal ball gaze" the future. They believe that if they and everyone else dug their heels in today, and gave this day the maximum effort toward meaningful goals, things would get done better and sooner.

Environmental Clues to Senser Type

- Desk: Cluttered and disorderly. Piles of papers, correspondence and projects in process. No apparent arrangements. Looks like chaos and disorganization.

- Office: Office will be in the same state as the desk. Cluttered with piles of papers and half-done projects. Might see two or three briefcases as well as a lap-top computer. Art work on the walls is likely to depict action or motion.

- Dress: Too busy to be neat. Simple in dress. Male Senser — jacket off, sleeves rolled up, tie loosened. Female Senser — something loose and casual. Few accessories.

SECTION II
DETERMINING YOUR PRIMARY AND BACK-UP STYLE
AND
THE EFFECTS OF STRESS ON EACH

HOW TO DETERMINE YOUR PRIMARY AND BACK-UP STYLE

Your highest scores in the squares—I, T, F, S—on the top half of the I-SPEAK Answer Sheet (FC Scores) refers to your primary style under normal or favorable circumstances.

The second highest score indicates your complementary or back-up style. While each of us uses all four styles, the lowest score on the top half of the Answer Sheet indicates that style least likely to be relied on by you under normal circumstances.

Illustration I:

I = 15	T = 27	F = 18	S = 30
Least-used Style	Back-up Style		Primary Style

In the above illustration, the individual's major style is SENSER. The back-up style is the THINKER style. Under normal conditions, the individual should behave in a very pragmatic, results-oriented and logical fashion. While being systematic in analyzing situations, the person may not place a premium on intellectual problem-solving for its own sake. For this type of individual, it is important to see concrete and tangible results. The person probably seeks activities which allow realistic and immediate feedback.

Style Shifts Under Stress

In Illustration I, the style least relied on, under normal conditions, is INTUITOR. Note what happens, in the illustration below, to the scores under circumstances involving stress.

Illustration II:

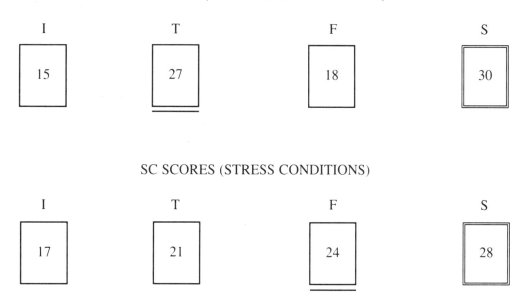

FC SCORES (FAVORABLE CONDITIONS)

I	T	F	S
15	27	18	30

SC SCORES (STRESS CONDITIONS)

I	T	F	S
17	21	24	28

Under stressful conditions, the individual still employs the SENSER style as the primary style. However, the back-up style, when stressed, shifts to FEELER rather than THINKER. Under normal conditions, the person is likely to be seen as down-to-earth, logical, controlled and somewhat impersonal in manner. Under stress, however, the person is likely to convey a less impersonal and unemotional impact. The individual will be more emotional, more personalized and more concerned about the feelings of others.

Now let us consider another illustration:

Illustration III:

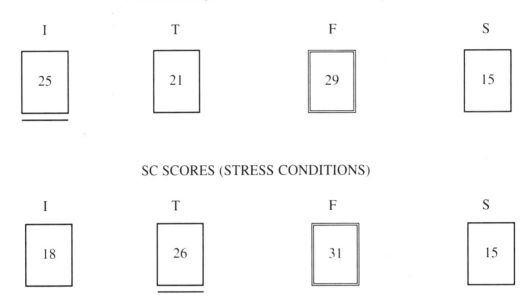

FC SCORES (FAVORABLE CONDITIONS)

I	T	F	S
25	21	29	15

SC SCORES (STRESS CONDITIONS)

I	T	F	S
18	26	31	15

This is the profile of a person whose primary style, under normal conditions, is FEELER and whose back-up style is INTUITOR — an individual to be seen as deeply involved in people-relations. Because of the secondary reliance on the INTUITOR style she/he is likely to be seen as lively, caring, warm but somewhat unpredictable. The person should be imaginative, idea oriented and concerned with basic causes and principles.

When in pressure situations, reliance on FEELER style remains dominant and even increases. However, the person is less concerned with the abstract or conceptual when stressed and relies more heavily on logic and planned problem solving, as the THINKER style. A boss might read the individual as being a good idea person, creative and concerned with raising far-reaching questions, yet is the type who will come through in the clutch as a resourceful performer in a crisis and under stress may be even more effective in selling ideas.

Illustration IV:

FC SCORES (FAVORABLE CONDITIONS)

I	T	F	S
19	28	20	23

SC SCORES (STRESS CONDITIONS)

I	T	F	S
21	25	15	29

This is the profile of a person whose primary style, under normal conditions, is Thinker and whose back-up style is Senser—an individual who is analytical and likes to examine a situation from all angles before making a decision. Under stress, this individual's primary style changes from Thinker to Senser, he/she becomes more action-oriented and the decision-making process moves more quickly than before.

What About the Spread Between Scores?

A difference of five points in spread between style scores, under either normal or stress conditions, IS SIGNIFICANT. A five-point spread suggests a clearly greater reliance on the higher score style. If the difference between primary and back-up scores is less than five points, the individual is likely to vary their style more readily. This, too, should NOT be considered positive or negative. Small differences in scores could suggest a high degree of flexibility and adaptiveness, but at the same time could suggest a tendency toward caution or indecision. Under normal situations or under stress, scores which are almost equal may suggest the following:

• The individual tends to be experimental in his/her approach to life and work.

• The person is still seeking a style that works best.

• She/he is self-critical and finds it difficult to rely consistently on any one style.

• Past experience has reinforced the value of shifting readily from one style to another.

• The individual adapts readily to circumstances of the moment.

SECTION III
OVERRELIANCE ON STYLE

It has been said that "any virtue carried to the extreme can become a crime." In fact, for most of us, our weaknesses are simply an overuse of our strengths.

Typical Cases

- The manager who has a keenly analytical mind but is so deliberative that he/she virtually becomes "frozen" when it comes to making decisions

- The sales professional who overemphasizes commitment to short-term volume targets on familiar products and disregards the potential of a new line

- The research and development engineer who "puts down" manufacturing requests for immediate machine modifications and only considers long-range projects essential to the corporate future

- The administrative assistant who is outstanding on planning office social functions, dynamic in telephone contact and helping colleagues solve problems has great difficulty in getting monthly financial reports in on time

Identifying the Real Problem

The above are illustrations of competent employees who encountered performance and/or relationship difficulties because they overrelied on their major style. However, the causes of their problems generally are not properly identified. Typically, these problems are viewed as representing conflicts between the opposing interests of different departments or as peculiarities of the employee.

• The R&D Engineer

If the R&D Engineer's boss successfully identified the problem of having a primary INTUITOR style and a back-up THINKER style, and recognized that manufacturing personnel demonstrated primary SENSER styles, a basis for improved relationships and teamwork could be established. Rather than intensifying the conflict by justifying his/her INTUITOR style, the engineer could concentrate on increasing the application of his/her back-up THINKER style and assist the SENSER to more clearly see and evaluate the practical value of proposed equipment changes.

• The Administrative Assistant

If the Administrative Assistant's boss deals with the problem of lateness as an expression of indifference, all we can predict is increased poor work, absenteeism and possible eventual termination. By employing the I-SPEAK communication system, the boss could indicate that the subordinate was overrelying on a FEELER style. By helping to reorient him/her to the job situation and make increased use of the less relied upon THINKER and SENSER styles, the employee could achieve a better mix of the various styles without becoming alienated as a result of the boss's attack on perceived time management issues.

Why We Over-stress One Style

There is always a reason for overreliance on a given style. Usually particular styles have been favorably reinforced by others. For instance, the manager in our previous illustration may have been commended for using his/her THINKER behaviors. Hence, the individual took pride in being pragmatic, "hard nosed," down to earth, mindful of cost control, conscientious in watching details, realistic in his/her approach, etc. Small wonder that the individual will use the THINKER style to excess. There is a fine line between useful THINKER behavior and overthinking behavior which causes people to pass judgment on the smallest details of subordinates' work.

What Can Be Done?

While it would be unrealistic to force an individual to alter his/her personality, it can be realistic to assist an individual to employ increasingly functional behavior. The I-SPEAK system attempts to diagnose style behavior, self-analyze and feed back behavioral observations to help each individual determine the extent to which his/her style applications are working constructively or not. It gives clear understanding of how overreliance on style or underuse of other styles may be contributing to difficulties in his/her work and life.

CHARACTERISTICS ASSOCIATED
WITH THE STYLES

	Effective Application	**Ineffective Application**
Intuitor Style	original imaginative creative charismatic idealistic ideological	unrealistic fantasy-bound scattered out-of-touch tenacious and dogmatic impractical
Thinker Style	analytical deliberative rational weighs alternatives stabilizing objective	overly serious, rigid indecisive overcautious overanalyzes unemotional controlled and controlling
Feeler Style	loyal persuasive empathetic draws out feelings of others probing introspective	impulsive subjective overpersonalizes sentimental postponing stirs up conflict
Senser Style	pragmatic assertive results-oriented technically skillful well organized objective—bases opinions on what he actually sees	short-range focus judging impulsive defensive nit-picking perceives loyalty as based on agreement

SECTION IV
OPPOSITIONAL STYLES

Frequently an individual may receive considerable benefit from close association with someone else whose primary style is opposite to their own. Thus:

An Intuitor Is Complemented By A Senser

- To help collect relevant data
- To ask questions of a specific nature
- To move back from long-range to immediate
- To recall specific details
- To design tests of an idea or theory
- To inspect or check
- To anticipate faults or criticism
- To translate strategy into timely, workable projects
- To "de-bug"
- To set up task forces, marketing networks, the machinery to make it happen

A Thinker Is Complemented By A Feeler

- To generate enthusiasm
- To reinforce, illustrate, dramatize ideas
- To help provide a light touch, humor
- To anticipate the reactions of others
- To assist in presentations
- To solicit viewpoints in advance
- To surface opposing ideas in resourceful fashion
- To teach others how a system or program works
- To sell a concept or system
- To reconcile differences, especially in emotionally charged situations
- To determine ways different media strategists can extend or reinforce a main message, concept or program
- To bring key people together socially
- To presell a new strategy, arouse interest and receptivity

A Feeler Is Complemented By A Thinker

• To act as a brake

• To assist in objectively considering all possibilities, not merely option(s) a Feeler is most enthusiastic about

• To identify and detail downside risks

• To assure that complete research, data, documentation is accomplished

• To organize and analyze

• To translate ideas into financial terms

• To criticize

• To test and weigh present plans against history and past performance

• To achieve consistency

• To anticipate factual expectations of others

• To compare ideas, programs, products, etc., with those of competitors

• To assist in "seeing" traits or behaviors temporarily screened out as a result of emotional factors

A Senser Is Complemented By An Intuitor

• To brainstorm a variety of alternatives and/or applications

• To see relatedness, i.e., product modifications, spin-offs, line extensions, etc.

• To project long-range consequences, possibilities

• To interpret the underlying thrust or intent of complex adversaries

• To deal with a multiplicity of complex and/or unsolved problems

• To determine the questions that should be asked, the issues to be addressed

• To assess the relevance of a product or service in the future

• To determine future problems, possibilities or opportunities affecting a present or projected strategy

• To catalyze otherwise conflicting viewpoints toward agreement on basic principles or concepts

SECTION V
I-SPEAK APPLICATIONS

KEY MANAGEMENT SITUATIONS WHICH CAN BE IMPROVED WITH THE I-SPEAK COMMUNICATING SYSTEMS APPROACH

Personnel Selection

Using I-SPEAK theory prior to an individual's employment can help your organization to:

• Avoid obvious poor fits or miscasting situations, e.g., hiring a strong INTUITOR for a very down-to-earth oriented position whose requirements emphasize the SENSER style

• Avoid blaming the employee for demonstrating style behavior which is not suitable within the organization

• Coach new hires on style behavior expected in a particular organizational role—helping an individual to see what kind of style shifts would be realistic and desirable

• Assist recruiters to become more effective observers of style behavior of candidates

• Assist top management to set specifications for key jobs, most effectively in light of the style patterns of existing executives with whom a new employee would have to mesh

The Manager-Subordinate Work Relationship

Frequently a manager and subordinate assume a certain work contract exists between them. When crises occur, they review basic expectations of each other and often discover that they both have a serious misunderstanding about their relationship. While I-SPEAK is not a substitute for the manager-subordinate contract, its use as a form of open communication can effectively reinforce and redefine the basic relationship. For example, assume the boss uses a primary INTUITOR style backed up by the FEELER style; subordinate recognizing his/her primary style is SENSER and his/her back-up is THINKER, this could help both understand and establish the possible consequences of their style differences when working toward a mutual goal. Such knowledge could pinpoint in advance possible sources of conflict or frustration between them. Such information could suggest ways they might use their styles to complement each other and to reinforce manners rather than be in opposition to one another or defensive.

Manager-Subordinate Coaching/Counseling

Usually it is easy for a manager to recognize a subordinate's performance difficulties, e.g., the subordinate works hard but fails to plan or prioritize; the subordinate identifies and analyzes alternatives but lacks a sense of urgency; the subordinate demonstrates strong skills in arriving at new concepts but is inattentive to detail and procrastinates. Even though the manager recognizes the problems, there may be frequent difficulty in helping the subordinate improve performance by job-coaching.

A major reason for this is that the manager is all too often likely to focus his/her attention on what is wrong rather than why it is wrong. When the boss focuses on what, he/she is more likely to coach the employee by telling and showing the subordinate what to do. Usually the subordinate already knows this. However, because the subordinate has not been helped to see why he/she performs inappropriately, he/she is likely to go on behaving the same way. Since the individual does not see how to change, it is hard to do so even if he/she wants to.

In a nonjudgmental way, the I-SPEAK system helps the manager to identify the primary and back-up style of the subordinate. The manager can evaluate the positive and negative behavioral implications of the subordinate's style. He/she will know which style behaviors haven't been previously stressed and need to be. He/she can learn ways in which the styles of the manager and the subordinate may mesh or conflict. Thus, the subordinate should be able to more clearly see that weak uses of certain functions may have represented an overreliance on his/her primary style.

Organizational Development and Team-building

In most management teams, consisting of one manager and 6-8 subordinates, much energy can be wasted as a result of conflicts and defensive behavior. These frustrations have less to do with basic fundamental differences than with difficulties in the team members' understanding style differences within the team. For example, the INTUITOR manager may feel the SENSER subordinates lack knowledge about long-range priorities. The THINKER subordinate could easily resent the FEELER manager with emphasis on analyzing the reactions of people before taking a course of action. As long as any one of these individuals maintains the position "I am right, you are wrong," the likelihood of conflicts and additional wasted time and energy will increase.

A KEY PRINCIPLE OF ALL COMMUNICATIONS SITUATIONS

Usually we respond most readily and favorably to communications which reflect our own styles.

Thus, INTUITORS place a premium on communications that are well thought out. They emphasize the central thought, principle idea or values, and do not waste time or space on details.

THINKERS will place a premium on communications which are well organized, systematic and logical in content. They emphasize facts, well-documented conclusions and specifics. Wherever possible, they will omit adjectives, judgments and feelings unless they have a specific bearing on the facts themselves.

FEELERS value communications that sound as though they came from another human being rather than from a machine. While they try to be factual and logical, they are not pedantic or fact-bound. They rely on illustrations based on real people in real situations.

SENSERS appreciate a specific and pragmatic approach. They do not like introductions, historical background, or verbal spaghetti. They are action-oriented, want to know what the other person intends to do or wants them to do, why, in what way, and for what purpose. They will minimize time and space for discussion, meetings and the like and thus they are certain of specific tangible outcomes.

SECTION VI
SELF-DEVELOPMENT EXERCISES

Suggested answers to exercises begin on page 44.

EXERCISE I
REVIEW OF BASIC I-SPEAK PRINCIPLES

1. The four basic personal styles — as described in I-SPEAK — are:

a.

b.

c.

d.

2. What style is most likely to be displayed by someone who is inclined to analyze situations carefully and to function in a logical orderly manner? (Check one)

a. ___ Intuitor
b. ___ Thinker
c. ___ Feeler
d. ___ Senser

3. The style most likely to be displayed by someone who places high value on action and thrives on getting things done is the style of a(n): (Check one)

a. ___ Intuitor
b. ___ Thinker
c. ___ Feeler
d. ___ Senser

4. Someone who is very effective in organizing himself/herself and encourages others to research and plan might be characterized as a(n): (Check one)

a. ___ Intuitor
b. ___ Thinker
c. ___ Feeler
d. ___ Senser

5. The style that is most characteristic of someone who likes to conceive and think in conceptual terms. This person is apt to be described in I-SPEAK as a(n): (Check one)

a. ___ Intuitor
b. ___ Thinker
c. ___ Feeler
d. ___ Senser

6. If you encounter an individual who places high value on human interaction and enjoys contact with others and the stimulation they provide, you would probably classify him/her as a(n): (Check one)

a. ___ Intuitor
b. ___ Thinker
c. ___ Feeler
d. ___ Senser

7. If you played the probabilities, in which of the following jobs would you most likely find the Thinker? (Check all appropriate responses)

___ Salesperson	___ Diplomat	___ Statistician
___ Lawyer	___ Philosopher	___ Accountant
___ Researcher	___ Author	___ Novelist

8. If you played the probabilities, in which of the following jobs would you most likely find the Senser? (Check all appropriate responses)

___ Photographer	___ Manager
___ Controller	___ Foreign Missionary
___ Construction Worker	___ Biologist
___ Professional Athlete	___ Lawyer
___ Airline Pilot	___ Salesperson

9. In which of the following jobs are we most likely to find one who predominantly uses the Feeler style? (Check all appropriate responses)

___ Entertainer	___ Newspaper Editor
___ Biologist	___ Retailer
___ Health Care Worker	___ Accountant
___ Auto Mechanic	___ Chemist
___ Supervisor	___ Technician

10. In which jobs are you most likely to find the Intuitor? (Check all appropriate responses)

___ Bond Trader   ___ Planner
___ Speech Therapist   ___ Manager
___ Researcher   ___ FBI Agent
___ Author   ___ Engineer
___ Cost Estimator   ___ Professor

11. Let's consider what can happen when people "overplay" their style or excessively rely upon it.

a. Someone gets irritated because others do not see the value of their ideas as they do. This person is likely to be a(n) _____.

b. Someone is seen as rigid or very cautious. He/she is likely to be a(n) _____.

c. Someone is seen as detached or being in an "Ivory Tower." This person is a(n) _____.

d. Someone makes quick decisions. He/she is a(n) _____.

e. If someone fails to see an issue in the same way, this person feels the other has not been loyal. This person is a(n) _____.

f. Someone gets concerned with departures from traditions—particularly if they have been successful in the past. He/She is a(n) _____.

g. Someone is subjective and impulsive. He/She is a(n) _____.

h. Someone's moods tend to fluctuate greatly. He/She is a(n) _____.

i. Someone is behaving rigidly, uncompromisingly and impractically. He/She is a(n) _____.

12. As to the issue of time and time orientation, check only one response to the following:

a. Thinks about the whole perspective of time — past, present and future.
___ Intuitor
___ Thinker
___ Feeler
___ Senser

b. Someone who is very much "here and now":
___ Intuitor
___ Thinker
___ Feeler
___ Senser

c. Someone who is oriented toward the future:
___ Intuitor
___ Thinker
___ Feeler
___ Senser

d. Someone who is oriented toward the past:
____ Intuitor
____ Thinker
____ Feeler
____ Senser

EXERCISE II
ANALYZING POTENTIAL PROBLEMS AND DIFFICULTIES

This exercise gives you a chance to examine the impact of your style on others and to also begin thinking about ways to modify your style in order to make your presentations most effective.

Let's consider potential problems you might have with others — particularly in presenting your ideas.

Move forward in this exercise until you come to the heading that describes your predominant style. If you have no primary style, or simply wish to test your understanding of all the styles, then try analyzing the potential danger of each style as it affects others.

INTUITOR

If you encounter a THINKER, in what way do you have to be careful so as not to turn him/her off?

_____
_____
_____

Suppose you meet a FEELER; you could turn him/her off because he/she may regard your approach as:

_____
_____
_____

You may turn off the SENSER, who is likely to regard your approach as:

_____
_____
_____

THINKER

If your primary style is THINKER, you may turn off the INTUITOR, who is likely to regard your approach as:

_____
_____
_____

You are likely to turn off the FEELER, who is likely to regard your approach as:

_____
_____
_____

You may turn off the SENSER, who is likely to regard your approach as:

_____
_____
_____

FEELER

If your primary style is FEELER, you may turn off the INTUITOR, who is likely to regard your approach as:

_____

_____

_____

You may turn off the THINKER, who is likely to regard your approach as:

_____

_____

_____

You may turn off the SENSER, who is likely to regard your approach as:

_____

_____

_____

SENSER

If your primary style is SENSER, you may turn off the INTUITOR, who is likely to regard your approach as:

_____

_____

_____

You may turn off the THINKER, who is likely to regard your approach as:

_____

_____

_____

You may turn off the FEELER, who is likely to regard your approach as:

_____

_____

_____

EXERCISE III
ANALYZING YOUR "SHORT SUIT" STYLE

The style upon which you least rely is referred to as your "short suit" style. Because we rarely display the behavior that is associated with this style, it is a clue to potential weaknesses or sources of conflict with others. For example, if your "short suit" is THINKER, we can speculate that you might be accused of being a "procrastinator" — of taking too long to get things done. The potential conflict that this can raise with the boss and/or others is obvious. Thus, it is very helpful to examine this least-preferred style and its implications for your effectiveness.

Think of a recent event in which you had a conflict (an argument, perhaps) with someone.
What was it about?

_____

_____

_____

Did this conflict have anything to do with your "short suit" style?__Yes __No

If yes, list two or three other persons who might react the same way to this style as did the person to whom you initially referred.

_____

_____

_____

How about the last time your boss (or spouse) criticized you? Did it have anything to do with your "short suit" style? __Yes __No

We need to pay more attention to this least-used style. List below two concrete, specific things you could do — without going overboard — to correct or compensate for potential deficiencies of not using this style more frequently. For example, the person with the "short suit" style of THINKER might decide to put together, each Monday, a schedule or plan for the key things that need to be done that week.

_____

_____

Name one person with whom you need to stress more clearly your "short suit" style.

List below what you might do, next time you interact with this person, to effectively use your "short suit" style.

_____

_____

31

EXERCISE IV
ERRORS YOU MAY COMMIT IN MAKING PRESENTATIONS

This exercise is designed to help remind you of the potential communication problems that are likely to manifest themselves during presentations.

Write below what possible things you might do that could detract from your presentations. (Considering your style, what might you have to watch out for when making presentations?)

EXERCISE V
A PERSONAL EXCURSION

1. Write in the space provided the name of a person you have trouble communicating with.

2. What is this person's primary style?

   What is this person's back-up style?

3. Write in the space provided three specific things you will have to do to "speak this person's language."

   _____

   _____

   _____

4. Now, try to talk this person into doing something that would be easy for him/her to do, but still be something that this person would not normally do.

I'll try to talk this person into:

5. TRY IT OUT!

6. Write here what happened (start at appropriate sentence):
a. I succeeded because

b. I failed because

c. I partially succeeded because

but I should have

to have achieved more success.

33

EXERCISE VI
PRACTICE IN QUICKLY DIAGNOSING STYLE OF OTHERS

Here are a number of exercises that enable you to practice how you may quickly appraise the communication style of the people you meet. You will be given an opportunity to make quick judgments on very small clues and then test out your hypothesis against the answers provided.

Telephone Contact

1. Suppose you talk with someone on the phone who does not seem particularly difficult to reach. This person does not seem very time-conscious nor interested in details. As you mention your idea or product, he/she may recall other products or ideas similar to yours and ask about the relationship between yours and the others. You ask for a meeting and he/she seems to grant it with some enthusiasm. The person is probably a(n):

Intuitor ✓   Thinker ___   Feeler ___   Senser ___

2. This time, the person does not seem particularly time-conscious either, but seems to consume much of your time. As he/she discusses some things about your idea or product, this person seems to talk considerably in terms of their possible application and appears somewhat casual about immediate specifics. This person is likely to be a(n):

Intuitor ___   Thinker ___   Feeler ✓   Senser ___

3. This person is difficult to get to, in fact, the assistant asked you a number of questions before you were finally put through. On the phone, he/she seems somewhat brusque and matter of fact. He/she asks how your product or idea has helped others in similar situations. Once you get his/her attention, the individual seems willing to set up a meeting time in the immediate future. The person is apt to be a(n):

Intuitor ___   Thinker ___   Feeler ___   Senser ✓

4. This person also seems hard to get through to. During the first contact, the assistant asked you to write a letter and then follow it up with your phone call. He/she seems quite distant on the phone, wants support data for your background and abilities, and is inclined to pin you down on some very specific facts and figures. This person is most likely a(n):

Intuitor ___   Thinker ✓   Feeler ___   Senser ___

At the Office

If you play the probabilities, additional data about the style of your contact can be gleaned from the way you are handled in the reception area:

1. The administrative assistant shows you in and even though your contact is waiting for you, he/she seems to be engaged in some other pursuit. You get the sense that you are interrupting some thought and that you are bringing him/her back to the immediate concern. This person is apt to be a(n):

Intuitor ✓   Thinker ___   Feeler ___   Senser ___

2. The administrative assistant comes to meet you and says that the person is tied up for the moment, but will be with you shortly. The person is apt to be a(n):

Intuitor ___   Thinker ___   Feeler ___   Senser _✓_

3. The contact comes out to meet you. He/she seems to be friendly and apologizes for being a bit late. The person is a(n):

Intuitor ___   Thinker ___   Feeler _✓_   Senser ___

4. The administrative assistant comes out to get you right on time. The person is a(n):

Intuitor ___   Thinker _✓_   Feeler ___   Senser ___

In the Office

	Possible Style
1. Contact's desk:	
a. Cluttered, a bit disorganized — books, magazines	_I_
b. Neat and tidy	_T_
c. Cluttered — project folders, unopened mail	_S_
d. Pictures of kids around — plaques, mementos	_F_
2. About the office:	
a. Charts on wall — computer printouts on table	_T_
b. Pictures on floor leaning against the wall, not hung up — files or piles of papers on the couch or credenza	_S_
c. Pictures on wall depict sailboats in storm	_S_
d. Room warm and colorful	_F_
e. Room a bit "offbeat"	_I_
f. No paintings or abstracts hanging on wall	_I_
g. Pictures of friends or family hanging up or on end tables	_F_
h. Much action and confusion — phones keep ringing	_S_

35

Appearance of Clothing

It is very difficult to draw conclusions from mode of dress; nevertheless, how and what a person wears does provide additional clues to one's personal style.

Possible Style

1. Simply, neatly dressed   _____
2. Unpressed skirt/pants   _____
3. Outlandish combination of clothes   _____
4. Conservative, understated suit   _____
5. Very stylish — well groomed   _____
6. Tie with small, precise design   _____
7. Jacket with nonmatching skirt/pants   _____
8. Well tailored — very neat appearance   _____
9. Appears very comfortably dressed   _____
10. Colorful clothes   _____

Reading Materials

Possible Style

1. On bookshelf is book FUTURE SHOCK by Alvin Toffler   _____
2. Textbooks or reference works having to do with topics related to contact's business   _____
3. Biographies, mixed with old and antique books   _____
4. A fair number of digests   _____
5. A number of business studies from the National Industrial Conference Board and various references with business reports and data   _____
6. A business newsletter lying on the desk or table — such as Kiplinger Letter   _____
7. Books of theories or principles   _____
8. Books having to do with human relations   _____

EXERCISE VII
PRACTICE IN QUICK DIAGNOSIS OF PERSONAL STYLE

Here are eight situations — some with obscure clues — to help you practice determining the style of others.

It is possible for many of the items to identify a strong back-up style. IF you can, indicate both primary and back-up styles.

1. You are chatting with one of your contacts. In response to the question, "How are things going?" the contact tells you about Sam, her boss. Because you enjoy people, you listen and try to figure out Sam's style. Here is how your contact relayed the story:

Sam usually wants things done right away, but he also has to be well grounded in fact. The staff tries to anticipate what is coming next and to do broad-gauge research as they go along. Most of the time it works and a storm is avoided. Sam threw them a curve, however, when he decided to update a vintage ad campaign for current use. Nobody had enough data, for one thing. Ben saved the day by dredging up statistics for each two-year period on one of the company's major product lines over the last twenty years and the sun came out again. Nothing ever bothers Sam for long, but he also does not like to hear many excuses.

What is Sam's most probable primary style? _____Senser_____

What is Sam's most probable back-up style? _____Thinker_____

2. The training manager comes out to the office area to greet you. You mention that Joe Doakes asked to be remembered to her and she brightens perceptibly. You follow her into a cheery office and note that she is a science fiction buff. There are several of the latest magazines and books on the subject. Framed illustrations from publications of the twenties and thirties hang over a glass case containing a number of imaginative "future" machine models that have been collected over the years.

What is the training manager's most probable primary style? _____Intuitor_____

What is her most probable back-up style? _____Feeler_____

3. Pat seemed to sound off at someone every ten minutes. He was under a lot of pressure, and maybe part of it was he didn't take the time to keep off other people's toes. Pat told it like he saw it and was not concerned with anyone else's feelings, or so it seemed. If you looked a little closer, you would realize that Pat's goal was to get the work out. His unit had a higher production record than most. Pat never stayed angry. Once the situation was corrected, things would go back to normal.

What is Pat's most probable primary style? _____SENSER_____

What is Pat's most probable back-up style? _____Feeler_____

4. You soon realize that what the customer really wants to see are comparative model changes for the past five years and any other bits of information you can give. You rifle your briefcase and serve up the comparative figures — prices — the works. At one point, the customer apologizes for putting you through so much trouble and launches into a lengthy description of how convenient it will be when we have fourth-generation banks of memory and can dial the information by telephone.

What is the customer's most probable primary style? _____Thinker_____

What is the customer's most probable back-up style? _____Intuitor_____

5. People were more awed than surprised when Lee's name appeared in the local paper. They'd been kidding her good-naturedly for all those years about the effort she put into the urban planning commission. Lee took it well enough and was always ready to reel off facts and figures to support her contentions. Obviously, Lee had done her homework, but it was hard to know what she was getting at. Now it all came out. Lee had been named to head a federally funded task force to plot the master plan for urban growth for the whole area. There was apt to be a lot of crow-eating among the neighbors.

What is Lee's most probable primary style? _____Intuitor_____

What is Lee's most probable back-up style? _____Thinker_____

6. The receptionist shows you in. In his shirt sleeves, your contact is standing at a window vaguely looking out as he speaks animatedly into the phone. He turns, waves you into a chair, and walks to a desk laden with computer printouts. Remarking pointedly into the phone that figures don't lie, he begins reading data into the receiver. His assistant, quietly confirming plane reservations on another phone, flashes an apologetic smile in an attempt to make you feel comfortable.

What is your contact's most probable primary style? _____Senser_____

What is your contact's most probable back-up style? _____Thinker_____

7. The new travel incentive plan had barely been announced before that johnny-on-the-spot Chris, a travel consultant, was after his first order from Chemsol. Chemsol had been a steady customer of the agency for five years, but had been lured to the competition. Now, Chris was quick to press the obvious advantages of the new plan to increase Chemsol's sales. Chris was elated when Chemsol bought the package and — typically Chris — came dashing into the office saying he wanted to share the good cheer by taking the staff out for lunch.

What is Chris's most probable primary style? _____Senser_____

What is Chris's most probable back-up style? _____Feeler_____

8. Mr. Wilson started the conversation by asking if you knew of several people in the community — people with whom he was associated in business. Apparently, he was trying to establish some common frame of reference. Mr. Wilson was also quick to point out the attractiveness of the suit you were wearing.

What is Mr. Wilson's most probable primary style? _____Feeler_____

What is Mr. Wilson's most probable back-up style? _____Not Enough Info_____

EXERCISE VIII
A CASE STUDY

Assume that you are Mr. Jones, a loan officer with a bank. Please read the following case, make some notes concerning your preliminary analysis and strategy, and then answer the discussion questions which follow.

One of your small customers for the past seven years, Mr. Carter, a generally outgoing, if disorganized individual, has suddenly had spectacular profit over the past two years. He makes bicycle tag plates and cereal manufacturers want more of the tags to put into cereal boxes for kids than he can produce. Mr. Carter has said he needs a large loan to buy new equipment to meet the demand. Because of your generally positive relationship, he contacted you and asked that you prepare some recommendations on the size and price of the loan. Mr. Carter said, "whatever you think would be good for me. You've talked to the equipment salesman. I want to get it going so we can equal production demand."

You developed some recommendations, but when you called to present them, you found that Mr. Carter had gone to Europe on vacation. For the next month, he was impossible to reach. He finally came to your office for a conference, reviewed your recommendations, but seemed unsure of himself. He left the meeting on a note of indecision.

You've called him twice since and he promised to get back in touch, but didn't. Three weeks ago, you reached him by phone and he stated that the family attorney, Ms. Smith, a woman whose reputation you know, had advised him not to make any investments at this time. Ms. Smith, who tends to be analytical and thorough, is known to be bearish on the future of business in general.

You feel impatient. You know you've got a good deal together for Mr. Carter. It all was very simple as far as you can see. You're annoyed by his indecision and you resent Ms. Smith's intrusion of herself into Mr. Carter's affairs.

You would like Mr. Carter to take some action on your recommendation without further delay.

1. What is Mr. Jones' style as the case depicts him? *SENSER   IMPATIENT*
   Reason: *Annoyed by indecision*

2. What is Mr. Carter's style? *FEELER   INDECISIVE, DISORGANIZED*
   Reason:

3. What is Ms. Smith's style? *THinker Analytical & thorough*
   Reason:

4. How may Mr. Jones' style have clashed with Mr. Carter's without his having realized it before?

5. How would you briefly analyze the cause of the present problem?

6. In light of the situation, what strategic plan might help Mr. Jones in this case and bring this interaction to a more successful conclusion?

EXERCISE IX
A CASE STUDY

In this case, assume that you are the pharmaceutical company representative, Mr. Carruthers.

You were attracted to your present position with Better Pharmaceuticals a year ago because BPI is a professionally oriented, sound company with good, well-tested products and a reputation for ethical practices. You have made two calls in the past six weeks on a physician who has just moved into your area. Dr. Brown was abrupt on your first visit, spent only several minutes with you, demanded some samples which you were unable to provide, and then hastily excused himself to get back to his patients. Two weeks ago, you called on him again and tried to reorient him concerning BPI and one of your better products. Dr. Brown was impolite, seemed disinterested, and interrupted you several times with pricing questions concerning other BPI products. When you answered his questions, Dr. Brown said he wasn't really interested in these products.

Finally, you said, "Dr. Brown, I am here to fill your professional needs and I am finding it difficult to do so. If I can really be of help and service, please tell me how."

This was his response: "Listen, Mr. Carruthers, where I come from, I got terrific deals from my suppliers. Plenty of free samples and ample price reductions, which I worked out informally, of course, with salespeople just like you. I might be interested in BPI's preparations 'A' and 'H', but I'd like enough samples for two months and then let's sit down and discuss a special deal."

Before you could respond, his nurse buzzed and Dr. Brown left, asking you to drop by in a week's time. BPI does not have a rigid policy against sampling, but discourages it as such practices have been abused by both physicians and some reps in the past.

1. What is Mr. Carruthers' style?   FEELER   HELP & SERVICE
   Reason:

2. What is Dr. Brown's style?   SENSER   Abrupt, impolite, disinterested,
   Reason: Interrupted.

3. How would you analyze the cause of the possible style conflict?

4. In light of this analysis, what strategic plan might you develop for the next visit to Dr. Brown?

EXERCISE X
A CASE STUDY

You are a consultant (primary style THINKER, back-up style FEELER) and you have called upon Chris Johnson, a prospective client, two or three times. While you have never done business with her firm before (a large marketing organization), Chris has always been receptive and seemed willing to listen to what you had to say. Thus encouraged, you called upon Chris from time to time, hoping to interest her in engaging you or your firm in a project.

Two months ago, you hit upon a topic that seemed of great concern to Chris: the rising turnover in support staff. You suggested a number of possible remedies, and, since Chris was interested, you asked if she would like you to submit a proposal. Chris indicated, "Yes, I would really appreciate your doing that."

You drew up the proposal and mailed it to Chris. Not receiving a response for two weeks, you called to inquire about it. Chris said that she was "interested" but had not really had a chance to make a yes-no decision. After asking if more details or information were needed, Chris responded by saying, "No, the proposal was quite complete and I am pleased with it." You waited another week and then called again with no greater success. You asked at that time if you couldn't get together for lunch to discuss the proposal and Chris willingly agreed.

During the luncheon discussion, you often tried to get a definitive answer from Chris about going ahead with the project. You had a very pleasant, amiable lunch, but Chris now seemed to indicate that "turnover" was not really such a significant problem, and she was trying to get a better feel for the essential issues. Chris wanted, for example, to evaluate the results of an attitude survey that was being done in the firm. She indicated, "Maybe there were multiple, underlying issues that were related to the turnover."

Frankly, you are quite puzzled about the situation. Chris has always listened to you, seemed concerned about the issues at hand, and also seemed to genuinely want to receive your proposal. Your proposal included practical means of overcoming most of the problems Chris was concerned about, so that the reluctance to move, despite what you are trying to say or do, is a puzzlement to you.

1. What is Chris Johnson's probable primary style?
   Reason: *Feeler   Amiable, friendly, warm — open to discussion*

2. Regarding Chris's communication style, what factors may be causing her puzzling reluctance to move ahead?
   doesn't want to hurt your feelings

3. Apart from communication style, what additional factors may be causing Chris's reluctance to move ahead?

4. What is the most logical step to take next?

5. What is it about your style that allowed this to happen in the first place?

SECTION VII
SUGGESTED ANSWERS TO
SELF-DEVELOPMENT EXERCISES

Answers to Exercise I:

1. Intuitor, Thinker, Feeler, and Senser

2. Thinker—Thinkers place high value on logic, ideas, and being systematic in how they go about looking at a problem. They also seem to find satisfaction in seeing to it that the most logical, systematic procedures are followed.

3. Senser—Sensers do not like time-consuming deliberations. They like looking to see things done and look for specific, concrete action on a here-and-now basis.

4. Thinker—Thinkers pride themselves on their planning and in looking at things in a logical, orderly procedure.

5. Intuitor—Intuitors place high value on ideas, innovation, concepts, theory and long-range planning.

6. Feeler—Feelers try to understand and analyze their own emotions and those of others. They have great concern for people, and, consequently, often have an excellent understanding of them.

7. If you picked lawyer, statistician and accountant, you are correct. All of these jobs involve a high degree of systematized and logical approaches to work.

8. Business professional, construction worker, professional athlete, salesperson, and airline pilot would all qualify under the Senser. All of these jobs involve making things happen on a here-and-now basis. They also provide opportunity for concrete, tangible results.

9. Entertainer, retailer and health care worker would be the most likely choices. Feelers are attracted to jobs in which social contacts are highly likely or where they are able to be sensitive to the needs and wants of others (entertainer, health care professional for example) Good supervisors also have a Feeler back-up style—particularly if they direct production line activity.

10. Planner, researcher, author (although novelist types are frequently Feelers) and professor. Intuitors like to be able to pull together groups and factions. They also are stimulated by broad-gauged, theoretical problem-solving.

11. a. Intuitor

    b. Thinker

    c. Intuitor

    d. Senser

    e. Senser. They believe that if they and everyone else gave this day their all, things would get done better and sooner—regardless of other factors.

    f. Thinker: When you try to deal with change—especially under pressure—they try rational principles that often seem rigid or dogmatic.

    g. Feeler (subjective gave it away)

    h. Feeler

    i. Intuitor (impractical was the key clue)

12. a. Thinker—usually likes to review back-up data, study it in relation to the present and then weigh alternative future courses of action.

    b. Senser—Often accused of not looking ahead to the long term. He/she has little patience with past history or background data.

    c. Intuitor—Thrives on situations that demand a long term point of view.

    d. Feeler—This is difficult sometimes to understand because the Feeler often appears concerned with what is happening "right now," but the Feeler is more oriented in the past in that he/she draws upon prior life experiences and relates them to the present.

Answers to Exercise II

Intuitor

May turn off Thinker because:
too broad brush, abstract, untested; a radical departure from the past; flaunting tradition, blue-sky, insufficiently documents

May turn off Feeler because:
intellectualized, theoretical, unintelligible; too complex; lacking in structure

May turn off Senser because:
idealistic; too free form in thought; ivory tower thinking and approaches

Thinker

May turn off Intuitor because:
cautious, lacking vision, belabored, repetitious, overly responsive to immediate constraints; unimaginative

May turn off Feeler because:
mechanistic, cut and dried; lacking enthusiasm, playing it safe, numerical; over-structured, lacking spontaneity; too formal, lacking a light touch, tradition bound, overly test-oriented

May turn off Senser because:
unnecessarily complicated; too research-oriented and insufficiently action-oriented. Overly analytical—insufficiently geared to the "bottom line"; hedging

Feeler

May turn off Intuitor because:
worrisome; overreactive; lacking in vision; too concerned with the feelings of others who demonstrate faulty judgment themselves; superficial

May turn off Thinker because:
impulsive; insufficiently thought through; not researched; relying on "gut feelings," not facts; lacking documentation; untested; proceeding on faith; having failed to weigh, delineate options

May turn off Senser because:
innovative, but impractical; more concerned with people's sensitivities than "hard bottom line" results; too free-form; blowing things out of proportion; more concerned with possibilities than action

Senser

May turn off Intuitor because:
too concerned with the immediate—this week, this month, this quarter; overly preoccupied with short-term results at the expense of long-term direction; opportunistic; not mindful of long-term objectives

May turn off Thinker because:
piecemeal; changeable; impulsive; lacking a systems approach; vague as to objectives and specific program phases; crisis oriented; lacking an orderly, sound business approach

May turn off Feeler because:
insensitive; task-oriented rather than people-oriented; using people rather than influencing them; authoritarian; insufficiently listening; too risk-oriented; not mindful of past loyalties and relationships

Answers to Exercise IV

If you are an Intuitor you may:
- be scattered in your comments—jumping about too much
- raise too many issues
- appear ego-centered
- be too lengthy
- appear rigid
- appear too judgmental
- appear condescending
- be too abstract
- concentrate too much on the concept; not enough on the how
- not really close

If you are a Senser you may:
- try to reach conclusions too fast
- not ask enough questions
- command
- jump in conversation and let the other person finish speaking
- be too aggressive—put listener on the defensive
- not take time to earn objections

If you are a Thinker you may:
- overexplain
- be too noncommittal
- be monotonic
- not express feelings enough
- ask too many fast questions
- want to lay out presentation in too rigid a fashion

If you are a Feeler you may:
- spend too much time talking about the past
- forget to cite facts
- oversimplify
- rely too much on your personality and not on data
- tell too many anecdotes or stories
- take too long to get to the main point of your presentation
- not push to bring objectives out in the open
- avoid bringing to the surface unpleasant facts

Answers to Exercise VI

Telephone Contact

1. Intuitor—Often responsive to a cold telephone call. The assistant may ask your identification, but is not apt to screen intensively. The person is probably going to respond best to low pressure, factual presentations combined with some imaginative suggestions that might catch his/her fancy.

2. Feeler—Of all the individuals, he/she is most likely to be responsive to a cold telephone call. You might try to set up for an informal meeting, such as over lunch, for example. The Thinker responds well when references are made about mutual friends and acquaintances. It is important, however, that you are not misled by casual friendly contact. Your lunch expense and time could easily be wasted on someone who is just curious to see what the market has to offer. Because he/she will not want to hurt your feelings, it may be hard for you to determine whether or not the person is really interested.

3. Senser—Obviously, the best approach to this individual is to quickly mention some immediate results that will come from your idea or product. It is best done in rather brief assertions.

4. Thinker—He/she is going to want a great deal of information. It is well to be prepared before you call so all the pertinent data is at your fingertips. The Thinker is going ⋅⋅ ⋅⋅⋅ ⋅ ⋅⋅ statements of fact, along with complete information.

At the Office

1. Intuitor
2. Senser—Usually busy with something else up to the last minute a⋅ thinking about you and your problem until you arrive at the scene. finish up other business before you can be ushered in.
3. Feeler
4. Thinker—He/she will have planned for you and will expect you to his/her schedule as well.

47

In the Office
1. a. Intuitor
   b. Thinker
   c. Senser
   d. Feeler

2. a. Thinker
   b. Senser
   c. Senser
   d. Feeler
   e. Intuitor
   f. Intuitor
   g. Feeler
   h. Senser

Appearance Clues

1. Senser—Likely to wear functional clothes
2. Intuitor—They don't care much about how they look
3. Intuitor—Likely to create their own style if they have any concern for appearance
4. Thinker
5. Feeler—Stylish because they like to make an impression
6. Thinker
7. Intuitor
8. Thinker
9. Senser
10. Feeler—Sometimes even flamboyant. Feelers often act on emotional feelings and may express their feelings with color

Reading Materials

1. Intuitor—Future probably gives this one away
2. Thinker—Look at their work as a study
3. Feeler—Biographies reflect interest in people
4. Senser—Prefer to have others do their reading for them, more inclined to read quick surveys
5. Thinker—Likes to compare reports; would probably rely on reference materials
6. Senser—Looks at summaries and is impatient; wants more definite and conscious material
7. Intuitor
8. Feeler—Human interest and human relations materials of interest

Answers to Exercise VII

1. Senser
   Thinker
2. Intuitor
   Feeler
3. Senser
   Feeler

4. Thinker
   Intuitor
5. Intuitor
   Thinker
6. Senser
   Thinker
7. Senser
   Feeler
8. Feeler
   Not enough information given to decide

Answers to Exercise VIII

1. Though difficult to diagnose, a good guess would be that the loan officer is a Senser. We get clues from the comment that he "feels impatient" and "is annoyed with the indecision" and resentful of the intrusion of Ms. Smith, whom Mr. Jones sees as someone slowing down forward progress.

2. Mr. Carter's style is Feeler. The fact that he is "disorganized" would probably rule out Thinker, and the fact that he would just drop the whole matter and run off to Europe on vacation would probably rule out Senser. In addition, we see Carter as being somewhat indecisive, since he has changed his mind and seemed not really interested in bringing the matter to a conclusion. Of the two remaining styles, Intuitor and Feeler, the probable conclusion is that he is primarily a Feeler. We also have some additional support from the fact that he did not really "call a spade a spade" in discussing with the loan officer his intentions not to proceed with the loan. A Feeler might not want to hurt someone's feelings and, therefore, would leave the meeting, as the case indicates, on a note of indecision.

   One final point: Mr. Carter's back-up style would be Intuitor. A clue comes from the description of him as "disorganized."

3. Ms. Smith probably is a Thinker. The clues we get stem from the words "very analytical and thorough"; other than that, it would be very difficult to characterize Ms. Smith.

4. Mr. Jones may have inadvertently clashed with Mr. Carter by taking a Senser approach to him. That is, he proceeded exactly as Mr. Carter asked, on a business-like basis, to prepare recommendations. However, Mr. Jones failed to establish the kind of relationship with the man that might have led to a stronger bond. Perhaps, for example, he did not inquire enough about the man's plans and personal life. If Mr. Jones had, he may have heard about the impending trip to Europe and, having learned of it, arranged to get the material together well before the vacation. Even upon Mr. Carter's return, built a stronger relationship. Also, he may have followed through.

5. The cause of the problem relates back to some of the style relationships. If, indeed, Mr. Carter is a Feeler, Ms. Smith, the Thinker, may appeal to him. Ms. Smith, who is described as analytical and thorough, probably sits back and discusses things at great length with Carter, and in that sense appeals to his Feeler needs for identification and closeness of relationship. Ms. Smith is also patient and does not "turn off" Carter by a brusque, businesslike approach to matters.

   Another cause of the problem is the implication by Mr. Jones that everything was "very simple." Few things in life are. In his direct approach to life, he probably does not allow himself to sufficiently look beyond the immediate and see some problems that, upon study, would become apparent. It may be true, too, that there is a bit of the Intuitor in Mr. Carter, and if Mr. Jones had been aware of this, he may not have dealt with simply the immediate loan problem, but developed a long-range plan of capital financing which would take into account future business trends, etc. It may well be that the lawyer's comments about a bearish future were taken very seriously by Mr. Carter because of his underlying Intuitor make-up.

6. The plan to make the interaction effective probably involves getting both Smith and Carter together. One that would appeal to Carter, and perhaps his Feeler make-up, would be to propose an informal meeting, perhaps over lunch, to discuss the situation and how the three of them might work together to optimize his business operations and to "plan for the future."

In this meeting, it would be necessary to deal with the lawyer's concern about the bearish future of business in general and recommend a more moderate expansion—perhaps with a small loan, but tying this into a long-range plan, which might involve ways of obtaining additional capital without much fuss (such as a line of credit as a function of profits or sales growth), and connect this in with your concern for perpetuating the business for the next generation of Carters, etc. In other words, we need to give Carter a personal, human reason for making sure his business remains viable and yet not overexpand. We also need to meet the Thinker needs of the lawyer by developing a long-range planning outlook as to how the bank will continue its relationship with the company and aid in its growth.

Answers to Exercise IX

1. It is difficult to state precisely the style of Carruthers. His inquiry to the doctor, however, in asking how he could be of "help and service" is a Feeler statement. Moreover, the fact that he seems somewhat concerned about the impoliteness and disinterest of the physician also might lend some support to the sensitivity aspect of the Feeler. Thus, in the absence of other data, we would probably conclude this to be his primary style.

2. Dr. Brown's style seems classic Senser. He is quite busy, works on close schedules, interrupts, seems impatient, has little time for things that he does not feel have immediate pay-out. He does not seem to have the sensitivity of the Feeler or the conceptual intuitiveness and theoretical orientation of the Intuitor, although he may have a back-up Thinker style. The last mentioned point is a fair guess since he completed his medical education—a scholastic program that includes many courses of a scientific-technical nature whose rigid methodology and logic Thinkers thrive on.

3. Assuming for a moment that this is a situation involving a conflict of personal style, one possible cause of the conflict is the basic Feeler/Senser conflict. The Feeler is upset and disturbed by the Senser's seeming arrogance, insensitivity and blatant concern for somewhat apparently selfish motives. The reaction to this is often one of rejection on the part of the Feeler, and, at the same time, the Senser sees the Feeler as not really concerned about the Senser's immediate problems.

Prompt response to the request for the samples on the first visit or some immediate follow through may have been helpful in talking the language of the Senser. Making his presentation in terms of excellent results and satisfied patients, as he presented his new products, might also have been helpful.

4. In terms of next visits, there are a number of options. One would be to get out on the table the basic differences between the two of them. It is vital to recognize the "here and now" results wanted by the Senser. Point out that you are "in tune" with his desire to increase his earnings, but also indicate quite frankly that there are ethical limitations on what the company can do in terms of price reductions or excessive sampling. You might point this out in the following way:

a. You understand his desire for favorable pricing and will work with him to the extent you can. Second, his time in the office might be more productive by a strong knowledge of one or two of your excellent products that have a high degree of effectiveness.

b. You will give him as many samples as you can.

c. You might point out that you want to come in and see him, that you recognize he is busy, will never take more than "x" minutes of his time, and will focus upon what the results have been and what other physicians have found. Let him make the decision then and there.

Answers to Exercise X

1. Chris Johnson's most probable primary style is Feeler. We judge this by the fact that Chris is quite amiable, friendly, always warm and open to discussion. Chris probably would go to great lengths not to offend or hurt anyone's feelings.

2. The problem occurring here is that Chris Johnson does not want to hurt your feelings. With your proposal, which probably is quite detailed, well organized, and obviously required considerable work, Chris may feel a bit guilty about telling you that she is not interested. In fact, it is only after considerable effort on your part that Chris finally indicated that turnover is not really the big problem. It would appear that if the assumption that Chris is a Feeler is correct, she is trying to avoid hurting you.

3. First, it may be that in your zealous desire to get a project, you latched onto the first problem mentioned and, in truth, turnover may not really be a significant problem in the firm. Thus, your proposal, while good, would not be seen by others as being a meaningful investment of your time and effort at this point.

   The second possibility is that you are talking with the wrong person. It may well be that Chris is not in a position to make the decision. Or, building on the same point, she may not have enough confidence in the proposal or herself to take it and sell it to others in the organization who can approve such a proposal. The final possibility might be that Chris has tried to sell this within the organization, has not met with success and does not want to admit this to you.

4. It would appear, in this case, that it is very important to now try and solicit the true objections to Chris's not going ahead. To do this, draw out the real reasons. If Chris is reluctant, then there is nothing wrong with suggesting possibilities. You might say, for example, "How do others in the organization, who would probably have to look at the proposal like this, feel about it as a means of overcoming a problem?" Or you could restate the entire scene and get Chris to elaborate upon it. You might say, for example, "I guess you're trying to tell me something here and that it is that you really would prefer not to go ahead with this proposal."

5. The key to this situation in the first place is that your back-up style is probably Feeler. Thus, you respond quite well to Chris Johnson, who is also a Feeler. Both of you enjoy interrelating with one another, enjoy the informal, friendly discussions. Neither one of you may probe sufficiently to find out the true problem and true reasons that exist. Thus there is a constant "sparring" about being the "nice guy" and not wanting to step upon one another's toes. If you are a Feeler in real life, it is quite likely that you will need to push yourself to surface unpleasant thought and comments—particularly when trying to draw out objections.

I-SPEAK
YOUR LANGUAGE®
A SURVEY OF PERSONAL STYLES

I-SPEAK Your Language® (I-SPEAK®) is a skill-building program that shows people how to determine communication styles (both their own and those of others) and teaches them to use this knowledge to foster enhanced communications and produce results.

The program is based on these premises:
- Individuals have recognizable and preferred communication styles.
- It is possible, after relatively short exposure to a person, to identify his/her style.
- People communicate most effectively with individuals whose styles are similar to their own and have greater difficulty communicating with people who exhibit dissimilar communication styles.
- People can modify their styles to "speak the language" of others.

There are four basic communication styles, and while individuals tend to exhibit features of each style, most favor and rely heavily on one. Reliance on a particular style often shifts during stressful situations. No one style is better or worse than another, as there are potential strengths and weaknesses associated with each.

When people understand their own I-SPEAK style and are able to recognize the styles of others, they can adapt their style to improve communication effectiveness.

I-SPEAK Your Language Materials

Several I-SPEAK Your Language components are available from DBM Publishing:

- The self-scoring **questionnaire** enables individuals to determine their own style.
- The **manual** illustrates each style in detail, explains when and how to effectively modify styles and offers practice exercises to further assist the individual in perfection of I-SPEAK skills.
- Two **videotapes** teach the viewer I-SPEAK style concepts as well as strategies for increasing their versatility. One video is geared toward upper-level, seasoned employees while the other works effectively with all levels.
- The **interviewing strategy** book shows interviewers and interviewees how to apply I-SPEAK principles to career transition situations.
- Style **buttons** add a visual and fun aspect to classroom training.

Steps in the I-SPEAK Your Language Process

I-SPEAK Your Language skills can be taught in individual or group settings. In either situation, participants begin by completing and scoring the I-SPEAK Your Language questionnaire to assess their own styles. No understanding of the I-SPEAK system is needed to fill out and tabulate the questionnaire. In fact, to insure that unintended biases do not creep into the personal assessment, <u>it is strongly recommended that the questionnaire be completed before any other materials are read.</u>

Next, participants move to the I-SPEAK Manual. Here they learn to interpret their scores to gain valuable insights into their own style. In the process, they are introduced to the characteristics of all four styles, learn how to recognize different styles in others, and study methods to use in a variety of situations to promote effective interaction with others having different styles. Self-development exercises in the Manual allow participants to continue to perfect their I-SPEAK skills on their own. The material focuses on using the system in different situations, allowing individuals to check their retention, and permits the participants to apply I-SPEAK Your Language principles to numerous real-life business situations.

The I-SPEAK videotapes, set in the culturally diverse workplace of the 90's, are an invaluable teaching tool. In addition to illustrating the four styles, they show styles in conflict and in harmony. Both the Upper-level and All levels videos help individuals visualize the I-SPEAK Your Language process in a number of on-the-job settings.

I-SPEAK Your Language has many applications including:

Management/Supervisory Development
Team Building
Self-awareness
Career Development
Job Search Skills
Sales Training
Conflict Resolution
Consumer Service Training

Ordering Information:
To order: call 1-800-345-5627
or fax 212-972-2120
or write: DBM Publishing
Order Department
100 Park Avenue
New York, NY 10017

About Drake Beam Morin, Inc.

Drake Beam Morin, Inc. (DBM) is the world's leading organizational and individual transition consulting firm. DBM provides organizations and their employees with the highest caliber services and products available in the areas of employee selection, performance, career and transition management.

For over two decades, we have assisted more than 70,000 organizations of all types and sizes and over five million individuals at all employee levels. The wealth of experience, which far surpasses any other firm in the industry, enables DBM to offer organizations the expertise that most effectively and efficiently meets their human resource challenges.

Through a network of over 150 offices around the globe, DBM provides personalized attention on a local level, along with a vast array of resources, wherever you may be located. With DBM, you have the best of two worlds: a local firm with a global presence.

To find out more about how any of DBM's programs can benefit your organization, contact your local DBM office or Marketing Services, DBM Corporate Headquarters, 100 Park Avenue, New York, NY 10017, 212 692-5813.

To receive our free products catalog, write or call:

DBM Publishing
100 Park Avenue
New York, NY 10017
800 345-5627